3D OBJECTS

Discovering Pyramids

Nancy Furstinger and John Willis

www.av2books.com

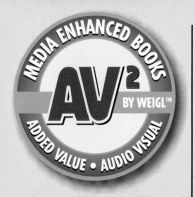

AV² provides enriched content that supplements and complements this book. Weigl's AV² books strive to create inspired learning and engage young minds in a total learning experience.

Your AV² Media Enhanced books come alive with...

Audio
Listen to sections of the book read aloud.

Key Words
Study vocabulary, and complete a matching word activity.

Video
Watch informative video clips.

Quizzes
Test your knowledge.

Embedded Weblinks
Gain additional information for research.

Slide Show
View images and captions, and prepare a presentation.

Try This!
Complete activities and hands-on experiments.

... and much, much more!

Go to **www.av2books.com**, and enter this book's unique code.

BOOK CODE

S 4 9 8 8 5 3

AV² by Weigl brings you media enhanced books that support active learning.

Published by AV² by Weigl
350 5ᵗʰ Avenue, 59ᵗʰ Floor
New York, NY 10118
www.av2books.com

Library of Congress Cataloging-in-Publication Data

Names: Furstinger, Nancy, author. | Willis, John, 1989-, author.
Title: Discovering pyramids / Nancy Furstinger and John Willis.
Description: New York, NY : AV2 by Weigl, [2016] | Series: 3D objects | Includes bibliographical references and index.
Identifiers: LCCN 2016005656 (print) | LCCN 2016012625 (ebook) | ISBN 9781489649836 (hard cover : alk. paper) | ISBN 9781489649843 (soft cover : alk. paper) | ISBN 9781489649850 (Multi-user ebk.)
Subjects: LCSH: Pyramid (Geometry)--Juvenile literature. | Geometry, Solid--Juvenile literature.
Classification: LCC QA491 .F8725 2016 (print) | LCC QA491 (ebook) | DDC 516.156--dc23
LC record available at https://lccn.loc.gov/2016005656

Printed in the United States of America in Brainerd, Minnesota
1 2 3 4 5 6 7 8 9 0 20 19 18 17 16

082016
210716

Project Coordinator: John Willis   Art Director: Terry Paulhus

Every reasonable effort has been made to trace ownership and to obtain permission to reprint copyright material. The publishers would be pleased to have any errors or omissions brought to their attention so that they may be corrected in subsequent printings.

Weigl acknowledges Getty Images, Alamy, Minden, and iStock as its primary image suppliers for this title.

CONTENTS

AT THE FARMERS' MARKET

You have helped your mother make preserved fruit. Now it is time to sell jars of oranges to hungry customers at the farmers' market. Stack the jars so they look nice. Each level of jars is smaller than the levels below it. Crown the top with the final jar.

You can stack many different things in a pyramid shape, including jars, blocks, and books.

The booth next door sells handmade toys. You pick up cloth juggling bags and toss them around. Did you notice the shape of the juggling bags is like the shape of the jam jar stack? Both of these shapes are **pyramids**.

Even plants can be shaped to look like pyramids.

WHAT DOES A PYRAMID LOOK LIKE?

Pyramids are all around us. Pyramids have three **dimensions**. These shapes are not flat. Flat shapes, like triangles, have only two dimensions, length and width. These flat shapes are also called **plane** shapes or 2D shapes.

Shapes that have three dimensions like pyramids are **3D** shapes. A pyramid's three dimensions are length, width, and height. We can measure all three dimensions. 3D shapes are also called solid shapes.

Sometimes, gemstones such as agate are carved into pyramid shapes and used in jewelery.

The *Pyramide du Louvre* is a glass-and-metal pyramid. It is located at the Louvre art museum in Paris, France.

HOW DO WE KNOW IF A SHAPE IS A PYRAMID?

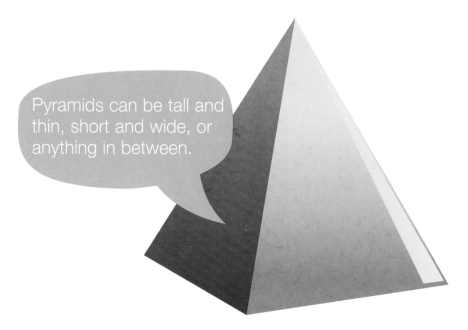

Pyramids can be tall and thin, short and wide, or anything in between.

Look closely. A pyramid has a flat bottom, called a **base**. Many pyramids have a square base. Some pyramids have a triangular base. A pyramid's base can even have five, six, or more sides.

Matching triangles form the sides of a pyramid. Each triangle is one of the pyramid's **faces**. These faces are two-dimensional flat **surfaces**. Each face forms a surface of a 3D shape. The faces come to a point at the top. The point is called a **vertex**. The place where any two faces meet is called an **edge**.

PARTS OF A PYRAMID

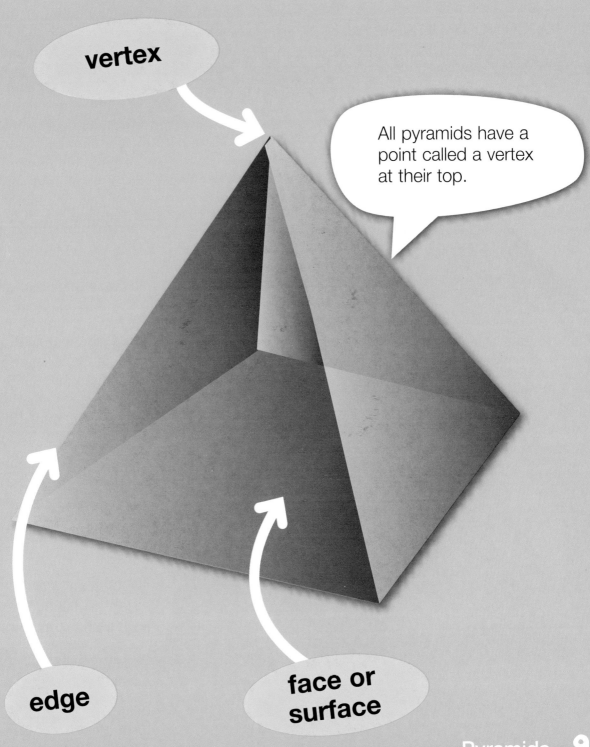

vertex

All pyramids have a point called a vertex at their top.

edge

face or surface

PLAYING IN PYRAMIDS

Once you know what a pyramid looks like, you will spot this 3D shape all around. You will start seeing pyramids in everyday objects.

Tents can have flat sides and a pointed top, like a pyramid.

At the library, there is a special tent with a pointy top. Inside, cozy pillows and a stack of books greet readers. Your family may have a tent almost the same shape. It has a square bottom with four sides sloping up. You may have slept in the tent when you went camping.

After reading, it is time to burn off energy on the playground. Climb up the jungle gym. Who will reach the pointy top first?

Some jungle gyms are shaped like pyramids.

THE GREAT PYRAMIDS

The world's most famous pyramids are in Egypt. Three pyramids rise above Giza, near the city of Cairo. The pyramids have lasted more than 4,500 years.

The largest, the Great Pyramid, once stood 481 feet (147 meters) tall. That is nearly as high as a 50-story building. Today, it is shorter. Some stones at the top fell off or were removed.

Pyramids were built to honor the Egyptian pharaohs, or kings. The kings' tombs were placed inside the pyramids. After death, the kings' bodies were preserved and wrapped in cloth. These mummies were buried with many things to help the kings live in the next world.

When scientists unearthed tombs in the pyramids, they discovered objects including jewelry, tools, food, and toys.

AN ANCIENT MYSTERY

Some secrets about the Great Pyramid remain to this day. Thousands of workers cut, moved, and then fit together more than 2 million stone blocks. Some blocks weighed as much as two elephants. How did the workers haul these blocks? Scientists today are not sure, but they believe it only took a few decades.

The ancient Egyptians' pyramids each have a square base and four faces.

PYRAMID BUILDINGS

The pyramid shape has inspired modern-day builders. A glass and steel pyramid greets museum visitors in Paris, France. Three smaller pyramids border the big one at the Louvre museum.

A stainless steel pyramid in Memphis, Tennessee, rises above the Mississippi River. The Pyramid Arena is the third-largest pyramid in the world.

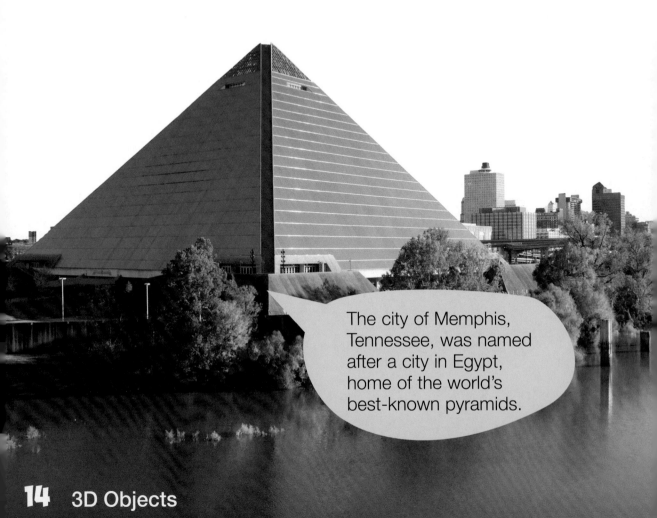

The city of Memphis, Tennessee, was named after a city in Egypt, home of the world's best-known pyramids.

SKYSCRAPER PYRAMID

Skyscrapers tower above San Francisco. The Transamerica building is the tallest skyscraper in the city. The concrete, glass, and steel building has a wide base. This helps it withstand earthquakes. At first, the builder designed a much taller pyramid. However, people worried this would ruin their view of San Francisco Bay.

The Transamerica Building is 853 feet (260 m) tall.

FLYING PYRAMIDS

A breezy day is perfect for flying your new kite. You made the kite using fishing lines, drinking straws, and tissue paper. Its pyramid shape helps your kite soar.

A famous inventor once made a similar kite. More than 100 years ago, Alexander Graham Bell wanted to create a flying machine. He used a strong frame for his kite. He named it *Cygnet*. It was a big pyramid made of nearly 3,400 smaller pyramids. The kite carried a pilot in the flight seat. *Cygnet* flew for seven minutes.

Flat kites are the most common, but they can also be 3D.

PYRAMIDS IN THE SAND

The beach is a lot of fun on a summer day. Today, there is a sand castle competition going on. Someone has built a copy of an Egyptian pyramid. In front of the pyramid is the Sphinx. The Sphinx has the body of a lion and the head of a person. People from ancient Greece and Egypt told stories about the Sphinx.

Build your own sand pyramid. Then, if you get hot, go under a beach umbrella. The umbrella is shaped like a pyramid, too.

PYRAMIDS IN NATURE

You can find pyramid shapes in nature. Some mountain peaks form this shape. Pyramid Peak in California looks like a huge, granite pyramid. Mount Rtanj in Serbia has the same shape. Some people believe aliens created this peak thousands of years ago, but scientists do not think that is true.

The taller Piton is 2,530 feet (771 m) tall, and the smaller Piton is 2,438 feet (743 m) tall.

Landforms called plugs form when **molten** rock from volcanoes hardens. Two of these plugs, the Pitons, are in the island country of Saint Lucia. The twin pyramid-shaped peaks rise above the Caribbean waters.

Search for pyramid shapes in your house or out and about. You will be amazed how many of these 3D shapes you can discover all around you.

There is also a "Pyramid Peak" in New Mexico. It is part of a mountain range called the Pyramid Mountains.

PYRAMIDS QUIZ

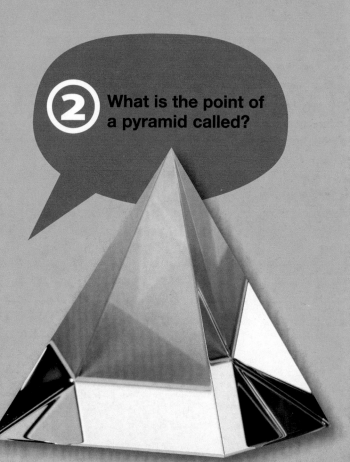

2 What is the point of a pyramid called?

1 Where is the *Pyramide du Louvre* located?

3 What are the pyramid-shaped plugs in Saint Lucia called?

4 How many stone blocks were used to make the Great Pyramid?

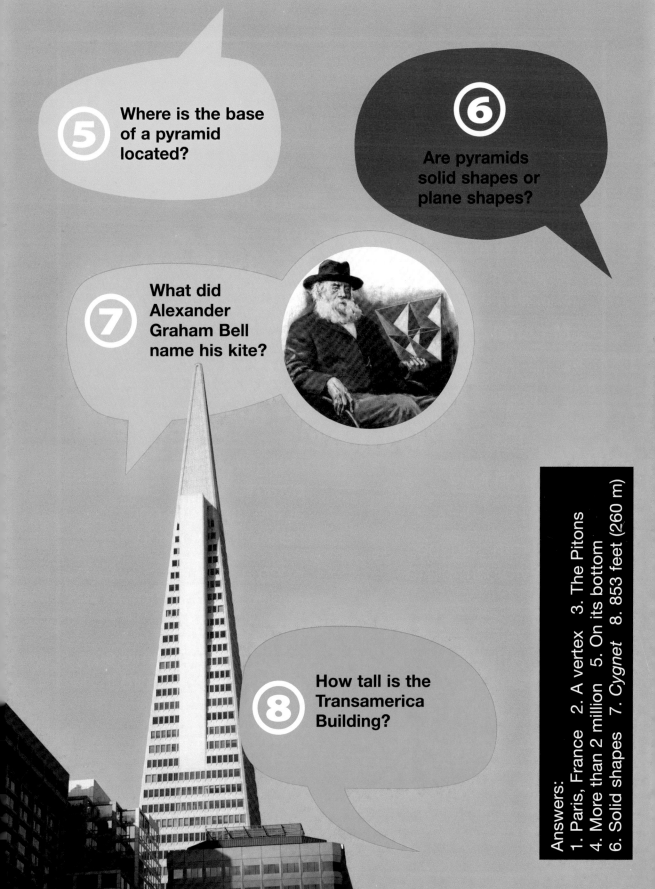

5 Where is the base of a pyramid located?

6 Are pyramids solid shapes or plane shapes?

7 What did Alexander Graham Bell name his kite?

8 How tall is the Transamerica Building?

Answers:
1. Paris, France 2. A vertex 3. The Pitons
4. More than 2 million 5. On its bottom
6. Solid shapes 7. *Cygnet* 8. 853 feet (260 m)

ACTIVITY:
PENNY PYRAMID

Save up your spare pennies to make this model of a pyramid. Then, display your shiny 3D shape in a special spot.

Materials

- pennies
- shallow dish
- salt
- lemon juice
- glue
- pyramid-shaped Styrofoam piece

Directions

1. First, make your pennies sparkle. Place them in the dish. Add a teaspoon of salt and pour in lemon juice until it covers the pennies. Wait a few minutes, then rinse and dry.

2. Once your pennies are dry, glue them to the pyramid shape. Start at the top. Glue one penny to each side.

3. Keep adding an additional penny to each lower row.

4. Display your pyramid so everyone can admire it.

KEY WORDS

3D: a shape with length, width, and height

base: a flat surface on a 3D shape

dimensions: the length, width, or height of an object

edge: the line where a surface begins or ends

faces: flat surfaces on a 3D shape

molten: liquefied by heat

plane: a flat surface

pyramids: 3D shapes with a base with three, four, or more sides that meet at the top in a point

surfaces: the flat or curved borders of a 3D shape

vertex: the point where the edges of a 3D shape meet

INDEX

Log on to www.av2books.com

AV² by Weigl brings you media enhanced books that support active learning. Go to www.av2books.com, and enter the special code found on page 2 of this book. You will gain access to enriched and enhanced content that supplements and complements this book. Content includes video, audio, weblinks, quizzes, a slide show, and activities.

AV² Online Navigation

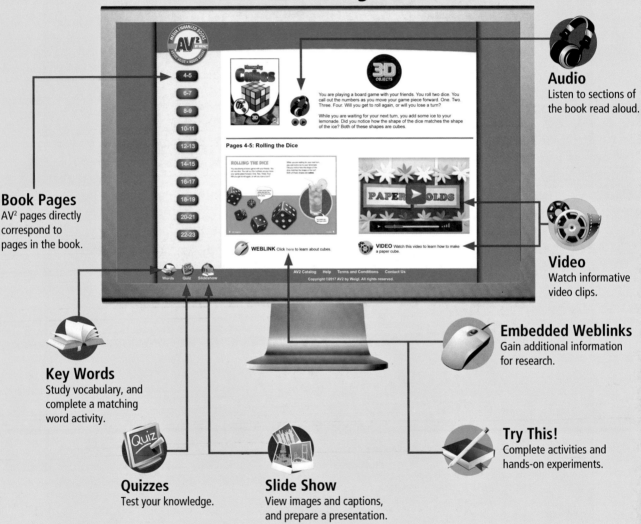

Book Pages
AV² pages directly correspond to pages in the book.

Key Words
Study vocabulary, and complete a matching word activity.

Quizzes
Test your knowledge.

Slide Show
View images and captions, and prepare a presentation.

Audio
Listen to sections of the book read aloud.

Video
Watch informative video clips.

Embedded Weblinks
Gain additional information for research.

Try This!
Complete activities and hands-on experiments.

AV² was built to bridge the gap between print and digital. We encourage you to tell us what you like and what you want to see in the future.

Sign up to be an AV² Ambassador at www.av2books.com/ambassador.

Due to the dynamic nature of the Internet, some of the URLs and activities provided as part of AV² by Weigl may have changed or ceased to exist. AV² by Weigl accepts no responsibility for any such changes. All media enhanced books are regularly monitored to update addresses and sites in a timely manner. Contact AV² by Weigl at 1-866-649-3445 or av2books@weigl.com with any questions, comments, or feedback.